971709

Daniel **R**adcliffe

Katherine Rawson

PowerKiDS
press.
New York

Published in 2010 by The Rosen Publishing Group, Inc.
29 East 21st Street, New York, NY 10010

First Edition

Editor: Nicole Pristash
Book Layout: Julio Gil
Photo Researcher: Jessica Gerweck

Photo Credits: Cover Jorge Herrera/Getty Images; p. 4 Alberto E. Rodriguez/Getty Images; p. 7 Dave Hogan/Getty Images; p. 8 Gareth Davies/Getty Images; p. 11 © Zuma Press Inc; p. 12 Scott Gries/Getty Images; p. 15 Don Arnold/WireImage/Getty Images; p. 16 Dave M. Benett/Getty Images; p. 19 Peter Kramer/Getty Images; p. 20 Alberto Rodriguez/Getty Images.

Library of Congress Cataloging-in-Publication Data

Rawson, Katherine.
  Daniel Radcliffe / Katherine Rawson. — 1st ed.
      p. cm. — (Kid stars!)
  Includes index.
  ISBN 978-1-4042-8135-6 (library binding) — ISBN 978-1-4358-3404-0 (pbk.) — ISBN 978-1-4358-3405-7 (6-pack)
  1. Radcliffe, Daniel, 1989– —Juvenile literature. 2. Actors—Great Britain—Biography—Juvenile literature. I. Title.
  PN2598.R27R39 2010
  791.4302'8092—dc22
  [B]
                                        2009007225

Manufactured in the United States of America

Contents

In July 2007, Daniel left his handprints in cement in front of Grauman's Chinese Theatre, in Los Angeles. Many of Hollywood's most famous people have done this.

Meet Daniel Radcliffe

Do you know who Harry Potter is? Harry Potter is a character from a **series** of books and movies about a boy **wizard**. If you have seen any of the Harry Potter movies, then you have also seen Daniel Radcliffe. Daniel is the actor who plays Harry.

Daniel's work in the Harry Potter movies has made him one of the most famous young actors of his time. He enjoys playing different characters in movies and on **stage**. "I am lucky enough to have a job I love," Daniel has said. Let's take a look at the life and the work of this talented actor.

A Young English Actor

Daniel Jacob Radcliffe was born on July 23, 1989, near London, England. His **parents** are Alan Radcliffe and Marcia Gresham. Daniel was interested in acting at a very young age. He got his first role, or part, in a school play when he was around six years old. He played a monkey!

A few years later, Daniel wanted to audition, or try out, for TV roles. His mother and father, though, were not sure if he should be an actor because he was so young. However, his parents finally let him audition. This would soon lead to great things for Daniel.

Daniel knew from a very young age that he wanted to be an actor. He used to act out scenes from movies at home.

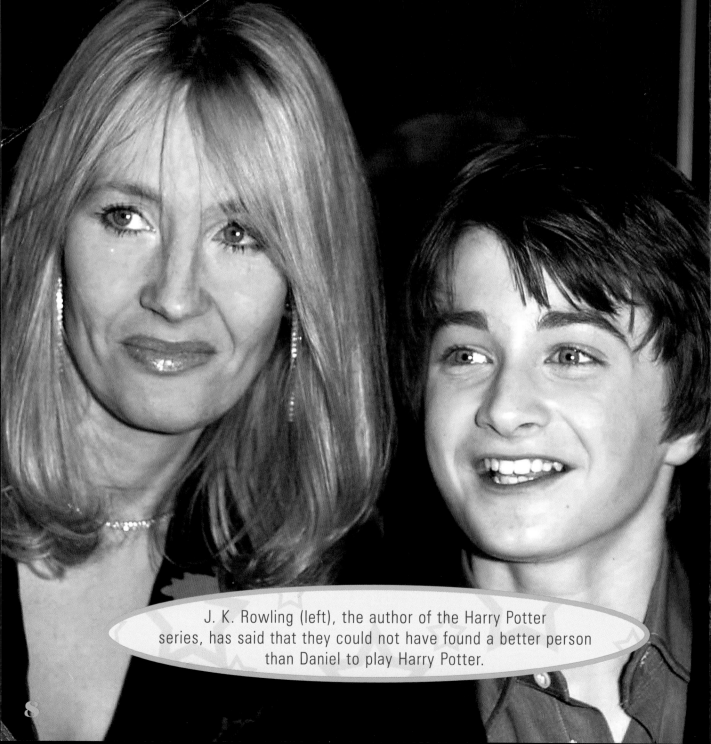

J. K. Rowling (left), the author of the Harry Potter series, has said that they could not have found a better person than Daniel to play Harry Potter.

Getting the Parts

In 1999, when he was 10 years old, Daniel won the lead role in the TV movie *David Copperfield*. He was very happy to get the part. After it came out, the movie's producer said Daniel was wonderful to work with.

Next, Daniel got a role in the 2001 movie *The Tailor of Panama*. He played the son of two of the lead characters. While Daniel was working on that movie, some moviemakers in England were searching for a special actor. They were looking for someone to play the lead character in a series of movies based on books by J. K. Rowling. That character was Harry Potter.

Harry Potter

The Harry Potter books are about a boy who finds out that he is a wizard. He is then sent to Hogwarts School of **Witchcraft** and Wizardry. The series follows Harry's years at Hogwarts. Chris Columbus, a movie **director**, saw Daniel act in *David Copperfield*. He wanted Daniel to audition for the role of Harry. Daniel's parents did not want Daniel to try out at first. However, they later agreed.

Daniel got the part. *Harry Potter and the Sorcerer's Stone*, the first movie in the series, opened in November 2001. The movie was a huge success. At 12 years old, Daniel's face was on **magazine** covers everywhere.

Here Daniel is seen with his costars from the first Harry Potter movie. Rupert Grint (left) plays Ron, and Emma Watson (right) plays Hermione.

In May 2004, Daniel went on MTV's *Total Request Live* to talk about *Harry Potter and the Prisoner of Azkaban*.

Hard at Work

Very soon, Daniel started working on *Harry Potter and the Chamber of Secrets*, the **sequel** to the first Harry Potter movie. *Chamber of Secrets* opened in 2002. Millions of people now knew who Daniel was. Two years later, *Harry Potter and the Prisoner of Azkaban* came out.

Acting in the Harry Potter movies was hard at times. For example, when Daniel acted in a scene with Dobby the House Elf, Dobby was not really there. The Dobby character was added into the scene later with a computer. When Daniel acted in the scene, he had to pretend that a stick was Dobby!

December Boys

The fourth Harry Potter movie, *Harry Potter and the Goblet of Fire*, opened in 2005. Some scenes in the movie take place under water, so Daniel had to learn how to **scuba dive**. His effort paid off. *Goblet of Fire* made more than $102 million in its first weekend!

Daniel enjoyed playing Harry Potter, but he wanted to try something different. In November 2005, at age 16, Daniel traveled to Australia to work on a movie called *December Boys*. Daniel played Maps, an **orphan**, in the movie. It was a different type of role for Daniel. It showed people that he could play many types of characters.

Here Daniel is shown with his castmates from *December Boys*. Daniel wanted to play the character Maps because it would require more effort than his other roles did.

Daniel enjoyed working with his *Equus* costars, shown here. He said that acting in the play was hard, but he loved having the chance to work with such great people.

On the Stage

After *December Boys*, Daniel started working on the fifth Harry Potter movie, *Harry Potter and the Order of the Phoenix*. Daniel did not stop there. Before *Order of the Phoenix* opened in July 2007, he was busy with a new job.

In February 2007, Daniel began starring in *Equus*, a play in London. This was a new type of character for Daniel. His character in the play is a troubled young man, not a schoolboy, as Harry Potter is. Many people were surprised to see Daniel in a role like this one. Daniel enjoyed it, though. "Being onstage and doing *Equus* was **fantastic**," he said.

Breaking Away

Daniel's next role was in the TV movie *My Boy Jack*. Daniel plays a young man who goes missing while fighting in World War I. Daniel liked that this movie had a simple story. He said that it was nice to break away from the magical story of Harry Potter to do a movie that was more realistic.

It would not be long before Daniel was onstage again. Daniel's role in *Equus* had been such a big success in London that, in 2008, the play moved to New York City. Daniel gained even more attention for the role and more fans as well.

Daniel learned a lot about World War I
while filming *My Boy Jack*. He has said that the story in the
movie was an important story to tell.

Daniel enjoys meeting and talking with his fans.
He says his fans are very important to him.

20

What's Next?

Harry Potter and the Half-Blood Prince followed by *Harry Potter and the Deathly Hallows* will be the last movies in the Harry Potter series. It will not be the last movie for Daniel Radcliffe, though.

The young boy from the first Harry Potter movie is now a young man. Daniel has had a lot of success, and his fans enjoy watching him. They cannot wait to see what he will do next. Daniel looks forward to trying new kinds of roles. We can expect to see him in many more movies. Daniel will continue to be one of the most famous actors around!

DANIEL RADCLIFFE

 When Daniel was a boy, he wanted to be a firefighter.

 English was his favorite subject in school.

 Daniel had not finished a Harry Potter book until he got his role in *Harry Potter and the Sorcerer's Stone*.

 Daniel loves rock music, and he enjoys playing the bass guitar.

 When he got the news that he had won the role of Harry Potter, he was taking a bath.

 Daniel once went to an all-boys school in London.

 Harry Potter and the Deathly Hallows is Daniel's **favorite** Harry Potter book.

 The Simpsons is his favorite TV show.

 Binka and Nugget are the names of Daniel's dogs.

 Daniel tries not to read any news about himself or his movies.

Glossary

director (dih-REK-ter) The person who tells movie or play actors what to do.

fantastic (fan-TAS-tik) Wonderful.

favorite (FAY-vuh-rut) Most liked.

magazine (MA-guh-zeen) A weekly or monthly grouping of pictures and articles.

orphan (OR-fun) A child or an animal who no longer has parents.

parents (PER-ents) Mothers and fathers.

scuba dive (SKOO-buh DYV) To swim underwater with an air tank on your back that is connected to your mouth by a tube.

sequel (SEE-kwel) A movie with the same characters and settings as an earlier movie.

series (SIR-eez) A group of similar things that come one after another.

stage (STAYJ) A raised platform on which actors perform.

witchcraft (WICH-kraft) Using magic.

wizard (WIH-zerd) A person with magical powers.

Index

A
Australia, 14

C
character(s), 5, 9,
13–14, 17
Columbus, Chris, 10

D
David Copperfield,
9–10

E
Equus, 17–18

H
*Harry Potter and the
Chamber of
Secrets*, 13
*Harry Potter and the
Sorcerer's Stone*,
10

L
London, 6, 17–18, 22

N
New York City, 18

R
Rowling, J. K., 9

W
World War I, 18

Web Sites

Due to the changing nature of Intenet links, PowerKids Press
has developed an online list of Web sites related to the subject
of this book. This site is updated regularly. Please use this link
to access the list:
www.powerkidslinks.com/kids/danielr/